Authentic Haitian Recipes

A Complete Cookbook of Island-Style Dish Ideas!

BY - Julia Chiles

Copyright 2020 - Julia Chiles

○○○

License Notes

OOOOOOOOOOOOOOOOOOOOOOOOOOOOOOOOOOOOOO

Table of Contents

Introduction

Most people in Haiti live fairly simple lives, and they often cultivate their own crops, which may include maize, sweet potatoes, bananas, beans or local coffee. They use the crops for their own meals and may sell extra crops in local marketplaces.

You'll need to find similar ingredients or suitable substitutes if you want your Haitian dishes to taste authentic. That's one of the goals of this cookbook.

Flavorful, spicy sauces are quite common in Haitian dishes. Among the favorite sauces is ti-malice, a spicy mixture of onions and tomatoes. The mid-day meal sometimes leaves leftovers for dinner, often made with porridge and fruits like mangos, pineapples or coconuts.

Haitians often dine on their national dish of rice and beans, and Sunday lunches typically include pumpkin soup. Other dishes use the most often used vegetables in Haiti, which include scotch bonnet peppers (hot hot!), other peppers, eggplant, beans, sweet potatoes and spinach.

You can find many similar ingredients in most areas, so it's possible to make dishes that are true to their Haitian backgrounds. Try some of these recipes soon!

Breakfast in Haiti is a time to relax and enjoy the morning tastes...

Corn Meal & Veggies

This dish, known as "Mayi Moulen" in Haiti, is a popular recipe for breakfast. You will mix up the ingredients, then cook them and mash them into a grainy consistency. It tastes better than it sounds!

Makes 3 Servings

Cooking + Prep Time: 45 minutes

Ingredients:

- 1/2 cup corn meal, fine
- 2 cups water, filtered
- 1/2 onion, chopped finely
- 1 tsp. of parsley
- 1 tsp. of thyme
- 1 tbsp. of oil, neutral
- As desired: garlic, kosher salt, ground pepper, hot pepper
- 1/4 bell pepper, red
- 1 carrot, medium
- Tomato, chopped, as desired
- 1 slice avocado
- Spinach
- Pepper, hot, as desired

Instructions:

1. Fry tomato, onion, carrot, bell pepper, spices and hot pepper, if using.
2. Add the corn meal and stir.
3. Pour in 2 cups water swiftly.
4. IMPORTANT: After you have poured the water, continuously beat mixture till cooked fully. This typically takes between 15 and 20 minutes. Don't stop till it is cooked.
5. Add spinach. Continue to beat.
6. Taste mixture. Season as desired and serve.

Haitian "French" Toast

This delicious, rich-flavored French toast is wonderful for either breakfast or a brunch. It is sometimes served with a variety of meats.

Makes 6 Servings

Cooking + Prep Time: 25 minutes + overnight sitting time

Ingredients:

- 1 baguette, French
- 1 cup of orange juice, fresh if available
- 1/2 cup of whipping cream, heavy
- 2 eggs, large
- 1 tsp. of cinnamon, ground
- 1/4 cup of sugar, white
- A dash of nutmeg, ground
- 3 tbsp. of butter, unsalted
- To dust: 2 tbsp. of sugar, powdered

Instructions:

1. Cut off baguette loaf ends. Cut the remainder of the loaf in slices of 1 & 1/2" thickness. Allow them to set overnight (8+ hours).

2. Combine cream, orange juice, cinnamon, eggs & white sugar in 13" x 9" casserole pan. Place the slices of bread in the pan. Turn till they absorb liquid, usually five minutes or so.

3. Melt the butter on med. heat in large sized skillet. Add sliced bread. Cook till browned on each side, five minutes or so. Generously dust with powdered sugar. Serve while warm.

Corn Flour Shake

This beverage is called "akasan" in Haiti. It's a shake with a base of corn flour. You can serve it warm, but typically it is placed in the refrigerator and served chilled.

Makes 2-4 Servings

Cooking + Prep Time: 35 minutes

Ingredients:

- 1 x 12-ounce can of milk, evaporated
- 2 & 1/2 cups water, filtered
- 1/2 cup flour, corn
- 1 tsp. Anise extract, pure
- 1 tsp. vanilla extract, pure
- 1/4 cup sugar, granulated
- 1/2 tsp. salt, kosher
- 1 tsp. cinnamon, ground

Instructions:

1. Bring two cups water plus cinnamon, salt & anise extract to boil in sauce pan.
2. Mix water and corn flour into paste in small sized bowl.
3. Add paste slowly to boiling water. Constantly stir so lumps are eliminated.
4. Reduce heat level to med. Allow flour to cook for four to six minutes while stirring constantly.
5. Remove anise star extract. Add evaporated milk and vanilla extract.
6. Thoroughly mix. Serve while warm or chill before serving.

Haitian Oatmeal with Nutmeg

Also known as "avwan" by Haitians, this is a favorite among locals. The recipe uses old fashioned rolled oats, along with nutmeg, cinnamon, butter and more. It's tasty!

Makes 3-4 Servings

Cooking + Prep Time: 1/2 hour

Ingredients:

- 1 1/2 cups of oats, rolled
- 1/2 cup of sugar, granulated +/- as desired
- 1/4 tsp. of salt, kosher
- 1/2 tsp. of nutmeg, ground
- 3/4 tsp. of Anise extract, pure
- 2 sticks of cinnamon
- 1 x 12-oz. can of milk, evaporated
- 1/2 tsp. of almond extract, pure
- 1 tbsp. of butter, unsalted

Instructions:

1. Add five cups water, cinnamon sticks and anise extract to medium sauce pan over high heat. Bring to boil.
2. Once mixture is boiling, add the milk, salt, sugar, oats and nutmeg. Mix thoroughly. Reduce heat and allow to cook for 12-15 minutes.
3. Add the almond extract and butter. Allow to simmer for 10 more minutes. Serve while still hot.

Papaya Breakfast Milk Shake

This milk shake is made from papaya juice, and it is a great start to any typical workday. It's quick to drink and gives you energy for your busy morning.

Makes 4 Servings

Cooking + Prep Time: 10-12 minutes

Ingredients:

- 2 cups of ice, crushed
- 1/2 peeled, de-seeded papaya, fresh
- 1 tsp. salt, kosher
- 1 x 12-ounce can of milk, evaporated
- 3 tbsp. sugar, granulated
- 1 tsp. vanilla extract, pure

Instructions:

1. Add all your ingredients to food processor.
2. Blend for two to three minutes. Chill and serve.

Haitians have all types of tropical dishes for lunch, dinner, side dishes and appetizers. Try one soon...

Haitian Beans Rice

This is an abbreviated version of the national dish of Haiti. It is adapted from their traditional style to make it easier to make. You'll love it with avocado served on the side.

Makes 6 Servings

Cooking + Prep Time: 2 hours 20 minutes

Ingredients:

- 1 x 8-oz. pkg. of kidney beans, dried
- 4 tbsp. of oil, olive
- 1 minced shallot
- 3 minced garlic cloves
- 1 cup of white rice, long-grain, uncooked
- 2 bay leaves, dried

Optional:

- 1 tsp. of adobo seasoning
- 1 tbsp. of salt, kosher
- Pepper, ground, as desired
- 1/4 tsp. of cloves, ground
- 3 fresh thyme sprigs
- 3 fresh parsley sprigs
- 1 pepper, scotch bonnet

Instructions:

1. Place the beans in large sized pot. Cover with three inches filtered water. Bring to boil and reduce heat.

2. Simmer for 1 1/2 hours, till tender. Then drain and reserve liquid.

3. Heat the oil in skillet on med. heat. Sauté the garlic and shallot till fragrant. Add and stir in the cooked beans. Cook for two minutes.

4. Measure the reserved liquid. Add water to make total of five cups. Stir this into the skillet. Add and stir in rice. Season using adobo seasoning, bay leaves, kosher salt, ground pepper and ground cloves.

5. Place thyme and parsley sprigs and the scotch bonnet pepper atop mixture. Bring to boil. Lower the heat and cover. Simmer for 15-20 minutes or so. Remove scotch pepper, parsley and thyme. Serve.

Haitian-Style Black Bean Soup

This soup is known as "sauce pwa" in the Caribbean. It is generally served along with white rice. You can make it with other types of beans, instead of black beans, if you like.

Makes 8 Servings

Cooking + Prep Time: 1 hour 40 minutes

Ingredients:

- 1 cup milk, coconut
- 16-ounce bag of beans, black
- 1 tbsp. of salt, kosher
- 1 tbsp. of pepper, ground
- 2 tbsp. of oil, olive
- 1 tsp. of cloves, ground
- 1 bouillon, chicken
- 8 cups water, filtered

Instructions:

1. Boil beans in water in large pot till soft, usually an hour or so. You can add extra water if you need it.
2. Once beans have softened, add 3/4 of beans to food processor. Puree with water from pot.
3. Run bean puree through strainer and return to beans in pot.
4. Add coconut milk, oil, kosher salt, ground pepper bouillon to pot, slowly stirring.
5. Cook beans over low heat level for 12-15 minutes. Serve over white rice.

Haitian Fried Chicken

This type of chicken has its roots in Haiti. It is different from the types of recipes you see in America and elsewhere, but you'll find it every bit as tasty. Leave it to marinate longer for the best flavor.

Makes 6 Servings

Cooking + Prep Time: 40 minutes + 12 hours marinating time

Ingredients:

- 3 lbs. of chicken legs, boneless
- 1 cup of lemon juice, fresh if available
- 1/2 chopped onion, white
- 1 head of garlic, with separated minced cloves
- 3 tbsp. of salt, seasoned
- 3 tbsp. of thyme, ground
- 3 tbsp. of paprika
- 2 tbsp. of pepper, ground
- 2 tbsp. of cloves, whole
- To fry: oil, vegetable

Instructions:

1. Combine chicken, onion, lemon juice, garlic, paprika, seasoned salt, thyme, cloves and pepper in large sized bowl. Cover. Marinate in fridge for 12 hours or longer.
2. Heat the oil in large pan on med-high. Fry the chicken in small batches till golden brown in color, eight minutes for each side or so. Drain the chicken in paper towels and serve.

Haitian Pumpkin Soup

This soup has a rich history, since it is a symbol of freedom from oppression in Haiti. Now it is enjoyed every January to celebrate freedom, and any other time of year.

Makes 8 Servings

Cooking + Prep Time: 1 hour 50 minutes

Ingredients:

- 1 pound of pumpkin, fresh or 12 ounces canned
- 8 cups of water, filtered
- 1 pound of stew meat, cubed
- Salt, kosher, as desired
- 1/2 tsp. of pepper, ground
- 4 crushed cloves of garlic
- 1 tsp. of thyme, dried
- 2 cloves, whole
- 1 chopped stalk of celery
- 1 chopped onion, large
- 2 cubed potatoes
- 1/4 chopped head of cabbage, small

Optional:

- 1 diced turnip
- 2 sliced carrots, medium
- 1 tbsp. of parsley, chopped

Optional:

- 1 hot pepper
- 1/4 pound of broken spaghetti
- 1 tbsp. of lime juice, fresh if available

Instructions:

1. Peel, then chop the fresh pumpkin coarsely. Add to a large pot with filtered water, stew meat, kosher salt, ground pepper, thyme, garlic, cloves, onion and celery. Bring to boil then lower the heat. Cover pot. Simmer for an hour or so, till meat becomes tender.

2. Remove the pumpkin from pot with a bit of broth. Puree in food processor. Return pumpkin to pot. Add cabbage, potatoes, carrots, parsley, turnip hot pepper.

3. Bring stew to boil, then lower heat. Simmer till veggies are nearly done. If you are using canned pumpkin, you should add it now. Add lime juice and spaghetti. Bring back up to boil. Cook for 10 minutes or so, till spaghetti has cooked. Remove the pepper. Season stew as desired and serve.

Haitian Sofrito

This vegetable and herb blend is used in Caribbean cooking for seasoning dishes with meat, rice or beans. The taste is very authentic – you'll love it!

Makes Various # of Servings

Cooking + Prep Time: 50 minutes

Ingredients:

- 6 various colored 1/4"-cubed bell peppers
- 10 cored, chopped tomatoes, ripe
- 1 chopped bunch of onions, green
- 1 1/2 chopped bunches of cilantro leaves, fresh
- 6 de-husked tomatillos, fresh
- 1 cup of garlic, chopped

Instructions:

1. Place various colored bell pepper cubes in bowl of your food processor. Add tomatoes, garlic, tomatillos, cilantro and green onions. Pulse or blend to create smooth or chunky mixture and serve with main dish.

Haitian Beet Salad

Have you ever had potato salad with beets in it? Probably not, and if you haven't, you're missing out on some serious good flavor. It doesn't look as natural as regular potato salad, but once you try it, you may never eat plain potato salad again.

Makes Various # of Servings

Cooking + Prep Time: 1/2 hour + chilling time

Ingredients:

- 2 beets
- 4 potatoes, red
- 1 diced stalk of celery
- 1/2 diced onion, medium
- 1/2 diced green pepper
- 1/2 cup of mayonnaise, reduced fat
- 1/2 tsp. of pepper, ground
- 1/2 tsp. of salt kosher, +/- as desired
- 1/2 cup of diced carrots

Instructions:

1. Boil the beets for five minutes in small pot.
2. Add potatoes. Boil for five more minutes.
3. Add carrots. Boil for five final minutes.
4. Drain pot. Allow potatoes and beets to cool.
5. Peel and dice the beets and peel and cube the potatoes.
6. Add all ingredients to large sized bowl. Mix well. Chill in fridge. Serve cold.

Haitian Turkey Meatballs

These homemade turkey meatballs from Haiti are simple, delicious and traditional. Usually, only one type of meat is used in each batch, and it is combined with spices. They taste great served with white rice or rice and red beans.

Makes 4-5 Servings

Cooking + Prep Time: 45 minutes

Ingredients:

- 1 1/3 pound of turkey, ground
- 1/2 minced yellow onion, small
- 1/4 minced green or red bell pepper
- 1 clove of garlic
- 1 tsp. of salt, kosher
- 1 tsp. of lime juice, fresh if available
- 2 slices of bread, white
- 1 tbsp. of parsley, chopped
- 1/2 cup of flour, all-purpose
- 3/4 cup of oil, neutral
- A sprinkle of pepper, ground

Instructions:

1. Mix the ground turkey with real lime juice, salt, chopped pepper, onions, chopped garlic clove and chopped parsley in large sized bowl.
2. Soak the bread in a bit of milk or water. Squeeze to remove excess liquid. Mix into other ingredients well.
3. Make about 15 ground turkey balls of 1 tbsp. each +/-. Roll them in flour. Heat pan with oil on med. heat.
4. Allow turkey balls to fry till golden brown in color. Turn and make sure all sides are browned. Don't let them burn.
5. Drain turkey balls in paper towels. Serve with tomatoes and lettuce or potatoes.

Haitian Accra Fritters

Fritters are a favorite appetizer or side dish among many native Haitians. It's easy to make, and cooks sometimes prepare a variety of accra, served in a "fritaille". You can just snack on them, too.

Makes 20 fritters

Cooking + Prep Time: 1/2 hour

Ingredients:

- 1 small-sized piece of chili pepper, hot
- 1 tbsp. of salt, coarse
- 6 peppercorns, whole
- 1/2 chopped onion, medium
- 2 cloves of garlic
- 1 egg, large
- 1 cup of malanga root, grated finely
- **To fry**: peanut oil

Instructions:

1. Pound pepper, salt, garlic, peppercorns and onion together into a paste.
2. Add this paste and the egg to the malanga root and beat till light.
3. Drop the mixture one spoonful after another into oil heated to 365F. Fry till golden in color and drain on paper towels. Serve.

Eggplant with Crab

The most popular crabs in Haiti are land crabs and soft shelled crabs. They have a taste that is pleasing, especially when combined with eggplant or other legumes.

Makes 6 Servings

Cooking + Prep Time: 2 hours 10 minutes

Ingredients:

- 12 cleaned, seasoned land crabs
- 6 sliced eggplants
- 2 pounds of spare rib or beef neck
- 1 pepper, scotch bonnet
- 10 ounces of peas, green
- 3 tsp. of salt, sea
- 1/4 cup of oil, vegetable
- 1/2 bell pepper, red
- 3 crushed cloves of garlic
- 1 lg. spoon of tomato paste, low sodium
- 4 tsp. of spices, ground
- 1 sliced onion, large
- 1/2 bell pepper, green
- 2 halved limes, fresh
- 4 sprigs of parsley
- 4 cups of water, filtered

Instructions:

1. Wash the crabs in cold water in large-sized container. Rub with one lime. Rinse them again. Season with 2 tsp. of ground spices.
2. In separate container, clean the meat with halved limes. Rinse off using cold, filtered water. Soak in hot, filtered water pre-boiled with 1/4 fresh lime. Discard the water after five minutes.
3. Season the meat using cloves of garlic, 2 tsp. of ground spices and 1 tsp. of sea salt. Allow to marinate.
4. Peel the eggplants. Slice in 1/2" slices in medium bowl.
5. Heat the oil over high in large sized pot. Add crabs, seasoned meat, 4 cups of filtered water and the eggplant slices for 40-45 minutes.
6. Remove slices of eggplant with a large sized spoon. Place them in separate bowl. Smash well.
7. When water in large pot evaporates, and the meat has turned golden brown in color, add the eggplant flesh.

8. Add the peas, onions, bell peppers, hot peppers, tomato paste, parsley and 1 tsp. of sea salt. Stir well. Lower the heat. Allow to simmer for 20-25 minutes.

9. Stir the mixture till water has evaporated. Season as desired and remove the hot peppers. Serve.

Callaloo

Callaloo has its origins in the Caribbean and is widely enjoyed in the region. It is made from indigenous plants like callaloo greens, and cooks often add foods from African recipes, like okra.

Makes 4-6 Servings

Cooking + Prep Time: 1 hour 15 minutes

Ingredients:

- 2 lbs. of crab meat, fresh
- 3 tbsp. of oil, peanut
- 3 minced scallions – include green tops
- 2 minced garlic cloves
- 1/2 tsp. of dried thyme
- 1/2-lb. of 1/4"-diced slab bacon
- 1 lb. of callaloo greens or fresh spinach – clean and remove stems
- 1 lb. of topped, tailed, sliced okra
- 7 cups of water, filtered
- Salt, sea
- Pepper, ground
- 1 chili pepper, scotch bonnet
- 3 fresh limes, juice only

Instructions:

1. Brown crab meat in oil with scallions, a tsp. of garlic and crumbled-up thyme.
2. Brown diced bacon in stock pot. Wilt spinach in rendered fat from bacon. Add okra and cover with filtered water. Add sea salt ground pepper as desired. Cook for 15-20 minutes while constantly stirring.
3. When step 2 is completed, add crab meat, the remainder of garlic and a chili pricked using a fork. Then continue cooking on low for 15-20 minutes while occasionally stirring.
4. When step 3 is completed, add lime juice. Whisk well. Serve hot.

Haitian Boiled Fish

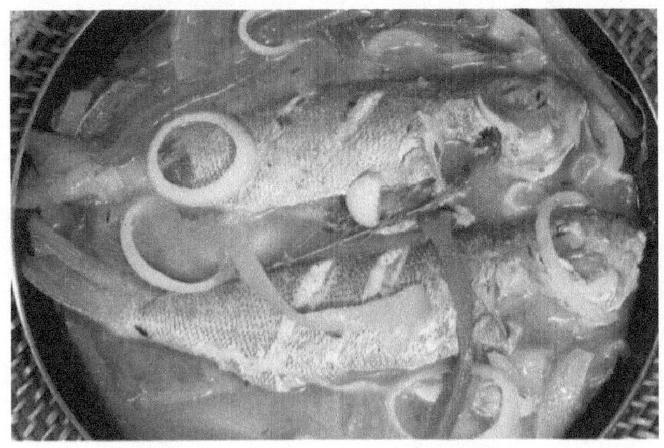

Red snapper or blue fish are usually used for this tasty dish. Fish are rich in many nutrients, and great care is taken to use only the freshest fish, which smell just like clean water.

Makes 5-6 Servings

Cooking + Prep Time: 45 minutes + 1 hour marinating time

Ingredients:

- 3 pounds of sliced red snapper or blue fish
- 1 onion, yellow
- 12 shallots
- 1 pepper, scotch bonnet
- 3 tsp. of salt, sea
- 1/2 cup of orange juice, sour
- 1 tbsp. of lime juice, fresh
- 1 tbsp. of vinegar, white
- 1 lg. spoonful of oil, olive
- 6 cloves
- 1/2 bell pepper, green

Instructions:

1. Allow yellow onions to soak in vinegar and 1 tsp. of sea salt.

2. Prepare, then clean the fish with halved limes, outside and inside. Rinse them with fresh water.

3. Marinate the fish with a mixture of OJ, minced bell peppers, onions, cloves, hot pepper 2 tsp. of sea salt for an hour or longer.

4. Add fish and marinade to large fry pan. Allow to cook both sides over low heat for seven to eight minutes. After they have cooked, carefully remove them to serving pan.

5. In separate fry pan, sauté onion and shallots in hot olive oil for two to three minutes.

6. Pour sautéed onions and oil over the fish. Garnish with shallots and lime wedges and serve.

Conch Fritters

This traditional recipe uses conch as its base. It's a delicious shellfish that is not found in many areas outside the Caribbean. These are wonderful for appetizers or you can serve them with your favorite Haitian tropical drink.

Makes 6 Servings

Cooking + Prep Time: 40 minutes + overnight setting time for batter

Ingredients:

- 1 1/2 cups of flour, all-purpose
- 1 1/2 tsp. of baking powder, sodium free
- 1/4 cup of green bell pepper, chopped finely
- 1/4 cup of red pepper, chopped finely
- 1/2 finely diced white onion, small
- 1 minced clove of garlic
- 1 tbsp. of parsley, fresh, chopped finely
- 1 tbsp. of fresh thyme, chopped finely
- 1/2 de-seeded, minced Scotch bonnet pepper
- 1/4 cup of milk, low-fat
- 3/4-lb. conch, chopped

Optional:

- 1/4 tsp. of salt, sea
- 1/4 tsp. of pepper, ground

To fry:

- 1 cup of oil, vegetable

Instructions:

1. Mix baking powder and flour in large-sized bowl. Add onions, bell peppers, parsley, garlic, Scotch bonnet pepper and thyme. Stir in the milk and beat the batter well. Add and stir in the chopped conch, sea salt, as desired ground pepper.
2. Allow batter to set in refrigerator overnight.
3. Next day, heat the oil to 375F in deep, large skillet. Cook fritters till golden brown and remove them. Drain on paper towels and serve with your favorite dressing.

Haitian Beef Vegetable Stew

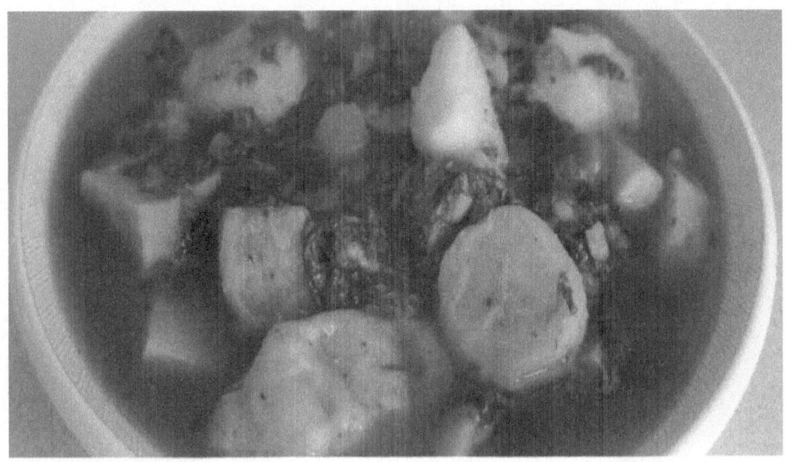

This vegetable and meat stew is easily made and very aromatic as it is cooking. It will fill your table for your family and guests, as a wonderful meal.

Makes 6-8 Servings

Cooking + Prep Time: 1 hour 35 minutes

Ingredients:

- 1 lb. of beef, cubed
- 2 fresh limes, halved
- 1 onion, large
- 4 chopped, crushed cloves of garlic
- 4 scallions
- 2 tbsp. of salt, kosher
- 1/2 tbsp. of pepper, black
- 2 bay leaves, dried
- 2 cloves
- 2 parsley sprigs
- 1 sprig of thyme
- 2 peeled, sliced carrots
- 2 sticks of celery
- 1 chunk-cut malanga
- 2 plantains, fresh
- 10 oz. spinach, fresh
- 1 yucca fruit

For dumplings

- 2 cups flour, whole wheat or white
- 1 tbsp. of oil, olive or vegetable
- 1 tsp. of spice, all-season
- 1 tsp. of nutmeg, ground
- 1 tsp. of pepper, cayenne
- 1/2 cup water, filtered

Instructions:

1. Clean the meat with hot water and lime.

2. Marinate the meat with kosher salt, ground pepper, garlic and scallions for one hour or longer in refrigerator.

3. As meat marinates, mix dumpling ingredients in medium bowl. Once they are mixed well, shape into dumplings and set them aside.

4. Brown meat with marinade in large sized pot on med. heat.

5. Add a quart of filtered water, bay leaves, cloves, thyme and parsley to pot. Continue to cook over med. heat for 40-45 minutes, occasionally stirring pot.

6. Add three quarts filtered water. Bring to boil.

7. Add celery, carrots, plantains, malanga, spinach and yucca. Cook for 20 minutes.

8. Add dumplings. Leave pot uncovered and simmer, unstirred for 20-25 minutes. Serve while hot.

Haitian Spicy Spaghetti

This slightly altered recipe is still true to its origins in Haiti. It uses tomato paste alone instead of combining it with ketchup, and you'll use vegetable oil rather than olive oil. This gives you much the same flavor with a simpler, quicker recipe.

Makes 6-8 Servings

Cooking + Prep Time: 40 minutes

Ingredients:

- 1 lb. of spaghetti
- 3 tbsp. of oil, olive
- 3 tbsp. of tomato paste, low sodium
- 1 tbsp. of garlic
- 1 cup of onions, white
- 1 tsp. of chopped thyme, fresh
- 5 sausages or other meat links
- 1 1/2 tbsp. of bouillon powder, chicken, reduced sodium
- 1 1/2 cups of water reserved from pasta cooking

Optional:

- 1/2 tsp. of crushed red pepper
- Salt, kosher, as desired
- Pepper, ground, as desired

Instructions:

1. Boil the pasta using package instructions.
2. Heat oil with tomato sauce in heavy, large sauce pan.
3. Cook and stir the tomato paste for three to four minutes.
4. Add sausage, thyme, onion and garlic. Stir while cooking for four minutes and blend well.
5. Add bouillon. Stir.
6. Add the pasta. Stir, blending, and add reserved pasta water gradually.
7. Lower the heat. Cover pan. Cook for four to five minutes more.
8. Add the crushed red pepper, as desired.
9. Season as desired and serve hot.

Haitian Watercress Salad

Watercress is a leafy green that is Vitamin-C rich and low-calorie. It boosts many types of Haitian dishes that include meatballs or fish. The greens are seasoned well so they won't soften and lose their appealing look.

Makes 1-2 Servings

Cooking + Prep Time: 55 minutes

Ingredients:

- 1 bunch of watercress
- 1 diced tomato, medium
- 1/4 cup of onion, diced
- 1/2 fresh lime, juice only
- 2 tbsp. of oil, olive
- A pinch of salt, kosher
- 1 tbsp. of chopped parsley, fresh
- 1 pinch of pepper, black

Optional:

- 1 tbsp. of honey, pure

Instructions:

1. Wash the watercress in bowl. Soak in lightly salted water for 20 to 30 minutes.
2. Remove woody stems and mushy leaves from watercress.
3. Rinse a couple times more with clean, fresh water. Pat it dry using paper towels.
4. In a separate bowl, add and combine onions and tomatoes. Add the lime juice, oil, parsley, kosher salt ground pepper.
5. Pour the dressing over the watercress. Mix well. Serve promptly. It goes well with seafood, meat or poultry.

Haitian Meat Okra Stew

This meat okra stew is sometimes made with fiery habanero peppers. This version is a bit tamer and uses more subtle vegetable flavors.

Makes 6 Servings

Cooking + Prep Time: 1 1/2 hours

Ingredients:

- 2 lbs. of cubed stew meat, mutton or beef
- 2 quarts of water, filtered
- 1/4 chopped cabbage head
- 2 tbsp. of oil, cooking
- 2 tbsp. of flour, all-purpose
- 1 chopped stalk of celery
- 2 chopped onions
- 2 dozen chopped okras
- 4 chopped tomatoes, large
- 1/2 tsp. of thyme
- As desired: kosher salt ground pepper

Optional:

- diced potatoes, corn or carrots

Instructions:

1. Combine the meat with cabbage in large pot of water.

2. Heat to a boil, then lower the heat and simmer meat cabbage till they are tender.

3. Heat the oil in heavy skillet. Then add the flour. Brown slowly.

4. Add tomatoes, okra, onions and celery.

5. Lower the heat. Cook and stir till all are tender, five minutes or so.

6. Add the veggies to your meat stock and then add the seasonings.

7. Leave pot uncovered and cook for 20 minutes more. Serve.

Haitian Spicy Coleslaw

Known as "pikliz" in Haiti, this is a favorite among natives. It is served with fried foods, pork, fish or beans and rice.

Makes 1 jar

Cooking + Prep Time: 15 minutes

Ingredients:

- 1 pound of coleslaw mix, tricolor
- 4 peppers, scotch bonnet
- 2 tbsp. of lime juice, fresh
- 1 tsp. of salt, kosher
- 1/2 cup of vinegar, apple cider
- 1/2 cup of vinegar, white distilled
- 1 bell pepper, red

Instructions:

1. Place all ingredients in large-sized bowl. Use a fork to combine well.
2. Place in airtight container. Refrigerator for two hours or so. Serve.

Sweet Potato Casserole

This tasty dish is a simple casserole to make, with a sweet Caribbean twist. Sweet potatoes, also known as batata, are very popular with many Haitian families. You can make the dish with yams, if you prefer.

Makes 4 Servings

Cooking + Prep Time: 1 hour 45 minutes

Ingredients:

- 2 lbs. of sweet potatoes
- 4 to 5 tbsp. of sugar, granulated, as desired
- 1/2 cup of butter, unsalted
- 1/2 cup of cream, light
- 2 beaten eggs, large
- 1 pinch of allspice or cinnamon
- To cover: mini marshmallows

Instructions:

1. Boil the sweet potatoes till tender. Peel off the skins. Place potato flesh in a mixing bowl. Mash well.
2. Add and stir in the rest of the ingredients, except the marshmallows. Combine well.
3. Spread the mixture into small, buttered casserole dish. Bake in 350F oven till middle has set. This usually takes 30-40 minutes or so.
4. Remove dish from the oven. Spread mini marshmallows on top.
5. Return dish to oven for several minutes, till marshmallows have browned lightly. Serve.

Haitian Oxtail Stew

This stew recipe **Makes** such delectable meat that it falls off the bone after it is braised. It's a Haitian comfort food that can be made easily in a pressure cooker, if you want to save time.

Makes 6 Servings

Cooking + Prep Time: 1 hour 25 minutes

Ingredients:

- 1 1/2 pounds of oxtail meat
- 1 x 15-ounce can of beans, Great Northern
- 2 sliced carrots, large
- 3 chopped garlic cloves
- 2 sliced onions, green
- 2 thyme sprigs
- 1/2 cup of chopped onions, yellow
- 1 cup of broth, vegetable or beef
- 2 tbsp. of Worcestershire sauce, low sodium
- 1 tsp. of cloves, ground
- 1 tsp. of pepper, ground
- 1 tsp. of salt, kosher
- 2 tbsp. of bouillon base, vegetable
- 2 tbsp. of oil, vegetable
- 1 tbsp. of glaze, culinary
- 2 sliced stalks of celery
- 2 chopped shallots
- 1 tbsp. of tomato paste, low sodium

Instructions:

1. Wash the meat and pat it dry. Set it aside.

2. In small bowl, mix Worcestershire sauce, cloves, glaze, bouillon, kosher salt ground pepper. Combine well. Pour this mixture over meat. Allow to marinate for at least 1/2 hour.

3. Click Sauté on Instant Pot. Set the timer for 15 minutes. Add oil and heat.

4. Sear oxtail meat on each side. Reserve marinating mixture. After oxtail has seared on each side, remove and place on plate.

5. Click on the Cancel button on Instant Pot. Sauté again for 15 more minutes. Add herbs and vegetables. Cook for five minutes or so.

6. Add tomato paste and then meat. Stir well. Add beans.

7. Add the broth and cover Instant Pot. Turn control to Sealing. Cook on high pressure for 45-50 minutes and serve while warm.

Haitian Lobster Curry

Natives of the Caribbean region were among the first to make lobster curry, which has many local variations. This simpler recipe uses lobster meat, where the older recipes used whole lobsters, which made more work.

Makes 4 Servings

Cooking + Prep Time: 45 minutes

Ingredients:

- 1 lb. of lobster meat, cooked
- 3 tbsp. of butter, unsalted
- 1 chopped onion, medium
- 2 tbsp. of curry powder, low sodium
- 1 chopped tomato, medium
- 1 cup of water or fish stock

Instructions:

1. Heat the butter in medium fry pan.
2. Add the onions. Sauté till they are soft.
3. Add and stir in the curry powder. Cook for a few minutes.
4. Add the tomatoes. Continue cooking for five minutes more.
5. Add the stock and lobster. Simmer till heated fully through.
6. Serve on noodles or rice.

There is always time for a treat
in Haiti. Try one of these
desserts soon...

Haitian Gingerbread

This dessert is known as "Bonbon Siwo" in Haiti. It's a wonderful treat made with brown sugar, cinnamon, nutmeg and ginger.

Makes 12 Servings

Cooking + Prep Time: 50 minutes

Ingredients:

- 3 eggs, large
- 2 cups of softened butter, unsalted
- 1 cup sugar, brown
- 1/2 tbsp. ginger, grated
- 1/2 tbsp. cinnamon, ground
- 1 tsp. nutmeg, ground
- 1/2 cup molasses
- 1 tsp. baking soda
- 1/2 tsp. vanilla extract, pure
- 4 cups flour, all-purpose

Optional: for the glaze

- 1/3 cup water, filtered
- 1 cup sugar, granulated
- 1 cup butter, unsalted
- 1 tbsp. rum
- 1 tsp. zest, orange
- 1 tsp. zest, lemon

Instructions:

1. Preheat the oven to 300F.

2. Beat together eggs, butter brown sugar.

3. Combine mixture from step 2 with remainder of ingredients in food processor. Beat into thick paste, with a texture like dough.

4. Spread paste in greased casserole dish. Bake in 300F oven for 45-50 minutes.

5. Set casserole dish aside. To prepare the glaze, if using, add water, butter, sugar and zest to sauce pan on high heat. Constantly stir for about 10 minutes till it caramelizes into a syrup that is semi-thick in consistency. Remove glaze from the heat and add the rum.

6. Drizzle glaze over dessert. Serve.

Cassava Cake

This Cassava cake is a traditional Haitian recipe. It's moist and soft, and the texture is a bit gummy. You'll love it after your first bite!

Makes 8-10 Servings

Cooking + Prep Time: 1 3/4 hour

Ingredients:

- 3 pounds peeled, grated yucca root
- 1 cup sugar, granulated
- 3 eggs, large
- 1 tbsp. rum
- 1 cup butter, unsalted
- 1 tsp. vanilla extract, pure
- 1/2 tsp. powdered cinnamon
- 1/2 tsp. grated nutmeg
- 1 can milk, evaporated
- 1 can milk, coconut

Instructions:

1. Peel yucca and cut off ends. Grate well.
2. Preheat oven to 350F.
3. Mix all ingredients in large bowl. Combine well.
4. Evenly spread batter into pre-greased pan.
5. Bake in 350F oven for 55-60 minutes. Allow to cool a bit and serve warm.

Coconut Treats

There are many vendors on the streets of Haiti that sell cocoye tablets, or coconut treats. It's a long-time favorite among native Haitians and it may become one of your favorites, too!

Makes 6-8 Servings

Cooking + Prep Time: 2 hours 35 minutes

Ingredients:

- 2 coconuts, whole
- 1/2 cup ginger root, grated
- 3/4-gallon water, filtered
- 4 sticks of cinnamon
- 1 tbsp. of cinnamon, ground
- 3 cups sugar, white
- 1 fresh lemon, zest only
- 1/4 tsp. salt, kosher
- 6 bay leaves, small
- 1/4 tsp. of vanilla extract, pure

Instructions:

1. Crack coconuts open. Scrape out white meat from shells.

2. Grate coconut meat into shreds in food processor.

3. Combine ginger and grated coconut in pot. Add filtered water. Bring to boil on high heat.

4. Add and stir in the sugar, cinnamon sticks and powdered cinnamon. Add bay leaves, kosher salt and lemon zest.

5. Reduce heat level to med-high. Cook for an hour while stirring occasionally, then increase heat again.

6. As consistency thickens, remove cinnamon sticks and bay leaves.

7. Constantly stir as consistency gets stickier. Add the vanilla extract.

8. After two hours in total, consistency should have become sticky and thick. Turn heat off. Transfer desired size of treats onto cookie sheet. Allow to cool for 1/2 hour, then serve.

Haitian Fudge

This fudge originated in Haiti, and it is known there as "Dous Makos". It sometimes contains layers made with food coloring for special occasions. At other times, it is served without the added colors.

Makes 8-10 Servings

Cooking + Prep Time: 1 hour 5 minutes

Ingredients:

- 2 cups sugar, granulated
- 1/2 cup milk, whole
- 1 x 14-oz. can milk, sweetened condensed
- 8 tbsp. butter, unsalted
- 1 tsp. of vanilla extract, pure
- 1/4 tsp. Anise extract, pure
- 1/4 tsp. nutmeg, ground
- 1/4 tsp. cinnamon, ground

Instructions:

1. In medium pot, mix all ingredients. Cook over med. heat while stirring constantly till sugar has dissolved.

2. After sugar has dissolved, raise the heat up to high. Continue to stir for 20 to 25 minutes, till mixture has internal temperature of 240F.

3. Remove pot from heat. Continue to stir for 10 to 15 minutes more. Mix will begin losing shiny color as it is cooling.

4. Place sheets of wax paper in mini-sized loaf pans. Fill with mixture.

5. Allow mixture to cool & harden for an hour or so.

6. Remove mixture from pan. Vertically slice and serve.

Almond Cake

This cake isn't overloaded with sugar, but it will still satisfy your sweet tooth. It's moist and dense. If you have Haitian rum, it Makes it more authentic.

Makes 8-10 Servings

Cooking + Prep Time: 2 1/2 hours

Ingredients:

- 2 1/3 cups of flour, all-purpose
- 1 tsp. of salt, kosher
- 1 1/2 tsp. of nutmeg, ground
- 1 tbsp. + 1 tsp. of baking powder
- 1 1/2 cups of sugar, granulated
- 3 eggs, large – separate and reserve the whites
- 2 sticks of butter, unsalted
- 1 cup of milk, evaporated
- 2 tbsp. of rum
- 1 1/2 tsp. of zest, lime
- 1 tsp. of vanilla extract, pure
- 1 tsp. of almond extract, pure

Instructions:

1. Preheat the oven to 350F.

2. Grease, then flour two x 9" cake pans and set them aside.

3. Sift flour, nutmeg, baking powder and salt together in medium sized bowl. Set bowl aside.

4. Add the rum to lime zest and set aside.

5. Use a mixer to cream the butter sugar in large sized bowl till fluffy and light. Add rum and the lime zest. Add the extracts. Mix well. Add egg yolks one after another and mix after each one is added.

6. Add milk and flour mixture gradually, alternating between one and the other. Mix till barely combined.

7. Beat the egg whites till they form stiff, fluffy peaks.

8. Fold the egg whites into the cake batter. Mix till barely combined.

9. Divide the batter into the two cake pans. Evenly spread. Bake for 25 to 30 minutes or till done.

10. Remove the cakes from your oven. Allow them to cool in refrigerator for an hour. Remove cakes carefully.

11. When cakes are completely cool, frost and serve.

Conclusion

This Haitian cookbook has shown you…

How to use different ingredients to affect unique tropical tastes in dishes both well-known and rare.

How can you include Haitian cuisine in your home recipes?

You can…

- Make cornmeal and papaya shake breakfast dishes. They are as delicious as they sound, and quite filling, too.

- Learn to cook with oxtail other meats, widely used in Haiti. Find it in meat departments of food markets.

- Enjoy making the delectable seafood dishes of Haiti, including lobster, bluefish and red snapper. Fish is a mainstay in the region, and there are SO many ways to make it great.

- Make dishes using plantains and yucca, which are often used in Haitian cooking.

- Make various types of desserts like gingerbread and Haitian cake that will tempt your family's sweet tooth.

Have fun experimenting! Enjoy the results!

Author's Afterthoughts

Thanks ever so much to each of my cherished readers for investing the time to read this book!

I know you could have picked from many other books, but you chose this one. So, a big thanks for reading all the way to the end. If you enjoyed this book or received value from it, I'd like to ask you for a favor. Please take a few minutes to **post an honest and heartfelt review on** *Amazon.com.* Your support does make a difference and helps to benefit other people.

Thanks!

Julia Chiles

About the Author

Julia Chiles

(1951-present)

Julia received her culinary degree from Le Counte' School of Culinary Delights in Paris, France. She enjoyed cooking more than any of her former positions. She lived in Montgomery, Alabama most of her life. She married Roger

Chiles and moved with him to Paris as he pursued his career in journalism. During the time she was there, she joined several cooking groups to learn the French cuisine, which inspired her to attend school and become a great chef.

Julia has achieved many awards in the field of food preparation. She has taught at several different culinary schools. She is in high demand on the talk show circulation, sharing her knowledge and recipes. Julia's favorite pastime is learning new ways to cook old dishes.

Julia is now writing cookbooks to add to her long list of achievements. The present one consists of favorite recipes as well as a few culinary delights from other cultures. She expands everyone's expectations on how to achieve wonderful dishes and not spend a lot of money. Julia firmly believes a wonderful dish can be prepare out of common household staples.

If anyone is interested in collecting Julia's cookbooks, check out your local bookstores and online. They are a big seller whatever venue you choose to purchase from.